The Secrets of Gingerbread

Its History, its Traditions, its Delicious Recipes

Joël Deberck

TABLE OF CONTENTS

INTRODUCTION

Welcome to "The Secrets of Gingerbread." This book is designed to celebrate a treat that spans ages and cultures: gingerbread. Whether you are a cooking enthusiast, a culinary history buff, a curious foodie, a family looking to share traditions, or simply someone interested in healthy eating, this book is for you.

We have embarked on this journey through the history and flavors of gingerbread with the humility of curious apprentices, always seeking to discover and share the culinary treasures of the past and present. We do not claim to know everything, but we have carefully gathered information, anecdotes, and recipes that we hope will enrich your knowledge and appreciation of this unique delicacy.

This book is a tribute to generations of bakers, pastry chefs, families, and gourmets who have continued and innovated this tradition over the centuries. We hope that our modest contribution will inspire you to explore, taste, and enjoy gingerbread in all its forms.

Whether you are a professional pastry chef looking for new ideas, a family preparing holiday treats, or simply someone wanting to learn more about a fascinating culinary tradition, we hope you will find stories, tips, and recipes here that will spark your interest and creativity.

In exploring the history of gingerbread, it is essential to understand the crucial role of spices. These precious ingredients, coming from all corners of the world, not only flavor and enrich gingerbread but also tell a rich story of discoveries and cultural exchanges. Let us now dive into the world of spices to discover their origins, production, and impact on this timeless treat.

Thank you for joining us on this gourmet adventure, and we hope you will enjoy reading this book as much as we enjoyed writing it.

Happy reading,

Joël

1 THE HISTORY OF GINGERBREAD

Ancient Origins

Gingerbread, as we know it today, is a treat deeply rooted in human history. Its origins date back to Antiquity, where the Egyptians, Greeks, and Romans prepared breads flavored with spices. These early breads were often used in religious rituals and offered to the gods as a sign of devotion. At that time, spices were precious and rare commodities, transported over long distances through perilous trade routes.

Imagine a freshly baked gingerbread, its intoxicating aroma of cinnamon and ginger filling the kitchen. The earliest gingerbread recipes included ingredients such as honey, cinnamon, ginger, and cloves, spices renowned for their medicinal properties. The Romans, in particular, valued gingerbread for its preservative qualities, making it perfect for long journeys.

With the fall of the Roman Empire, the knowledge of gingerbread spread throughout Europe, evolving and adapting to local tastes and ingredients. The Middle Ages saw the rise of gingerbread in monasteries, where monks continued the tradition of this pastry, using spices to mask the taste of poor-quality flour.

Welcome to our culinary journey through time. Gingerbread represents a rich connection to our ancestors and their traditions. We have explored centuries of practices to bring you the best recipes and anecdotes about gingerbread, a treat that deeply fascinates us. We hope that our modest contribution will inspire you to explore, taste, and enjoy gingerbread in all its forms.

Development in Europe

As the knowledge of gingerbread spread throughout Europe following the fall of the Roman Empire, each region brought its own touch to this fragrant treat. In Germany, the city of Nuremberg became famous for its *Lebkuchen*, a particularly prized variety of gingerbread. As early as the 13th century, Nuremberg was a thriving trade center located on major trade routes that facilitated the supply of rare and precious spices.

The bakers of Nuremberg, benefiting from this abundance of spices, perfected the gingerbread recipe by adding almonds, hazelnuts, and candied fruits, creating a rich and complex version of this pastry. Nuremberg's *Lebkuchen* quickly gained renown and became a staple of German Christmas markets, a tradition that continues to this day.

Lebkuchen from Nuremberg

In France, it is in the city of Dijon that gingerbread found a warm home. Introduced by the Crusaders returning from the East, Dijon gingerbread evolved to become a regional specialty. The traditional Burgundy recipe highlights local honey and a blend of spices that includes cinnamon, anise, and ginger. "*Pain d'épices de Dijon*" is cherished for its soft texture and subtle flavors, and it is often enjoyed with a glass of mulled wine during the winter months.

Pain d'épices de Dijon

Italy, on the other hand, developed its own version of gingerbread called *Panforte*, originating from Siena. *Panforte* is a dense and rich cake made with honey, dried fruits, nuts, and spices such as cinnamon and black pepper. Traditionally consumed during the holiday season, *Panforte* is often wrapped in rice paper and appreciated for its long shelf life, making it an ideal gift to give.

In the United Kingdom, gingerbread is known as gingerbread. Introduced in the 12th century by knights returning from the Crusades, British gingerbread evolved into a delicious festive pastry. The famous gingerbread men appeared at the court of Queen Elizabeth I, who had biscuits made in the likeness of her distinguished guests.

Panforte from Sienne

Gingerbread men

Each region of Europe has thus contributed to the evolution and diversification of gingerbread, adapting to local tastes and ingredients. This diversity has enriched the European culinary heritage, making gingerbread a cherished and celebrated treat across the continent.

The Evolution of the Recipe through the Ages

Over the centuries, the recipe for gingerbread has continually evolved, influenced by the discovery of new ingredients, culinary innovations, and cultural exchanges. The modifications made to the original recipe have allowed for the creation of a variety of gingerbreads adapted to the tastes and preferences of each era and region.

In the Middle Ages, European monasteries played a key role in preserving and transmitting the gingerbread recipe. The monks, skilled in the art of baking, perfected the preparation technique using local spices and ingredients. Honey, an essential ingredient of gingerbread, was often produced in monastic beekeepers, ensuring a constant and high-quality supply.

During the Renaissance, trade exchanges with the East introduced new spices and ingredients to Europe, enriching the flavor palette of gingerbread. Sugar, sourced from colonial sugarcane plantations, gradually replaced honey in some recipes, offering a different texture and sweetness. Candied fruits, nuts, and almonds also appeared, adding additional dimensions to the taste and texture of gingerbread.

The 17th and 18th centuries marked a period of culinary innovation, with the rise of pastry as a refined art. Bakers and pastry chefs experimented with various spices and ingredients to create unique versions of gingerbread. Baking techniques also improved, allowing for the production of softer and better-preserved gingerbreads. It was during this period that decorative forms of gingerbread, such as gingerbread houses and figurines, became popular, particularly in Germany and Alsace.

In the 19th century, industrialization transformed gingerbread production. Steam mills and modern ovens allowed for larger-scale production while ensuring consistent quality. Traditional recipes were adapted to meet consumer needs, and gingerbread became a treat accessible to a wider audience. Cookbooks of the time were filled with gingerbread recipes, testifying to its growing popularity.

In the 20th century, gingerbread continued to evolve, influenced by food trends and consumer preferences. Modern recipes often incorporate exotic ingredients and flavor variations, such as chocolate, citrus fruits, and spices from other continents. Gingerbread has also found its place in haute cuisine, where renowned chefs reinvent it to create sophisticated and innovative desserts.

Today, gingerbread is a versatile treat that continues to captivate pastry lovers worldwide. Whether in its traditional form or modernized versions, gingerbread remains a symbol of conviviality and sharing, crossing the ages with its comforting aromas and spicy flavors.

Gingerbread and Its Cultural Influences

Gingerbread, much more than a simple delicacy, has permeated the cultures and traditions of many societies throughout the ages. Each region that has adopted it has brought its own influence, making gingerbread a true reflection of cultural exchanges and local traditions.

In Europe, gingerbread is often associated with religious celebrations and popular festivals. In Germany, for example, the famous Christmas markets (*Weihnachtsmärkte*) are incomplete without the stalls selling *Lebkuchen*, created in Nuremberg as previously mentioned, and *Pfefferkuchen*, gingerbreads often decorated with festive patterns. These treats are also given as gifts, symbolizing the warmth and conviviality of the holiday season.

Christmas market in Germany

In France, gingerbread is closely associated with certain regions such as Burgundy and Alsace. In Dijon, gingerbread is a symbol of the local culinary heritage, often enjoyed with regional specialties such as mulled wine. In Alsace, *Bredele*, small Christmas cookies, often include gingerbread variations, highlighting the importance of this treat in Alsatian festive traditions.

Bredele from Alsace

In Scandinavia, gingerbread takes the form of *Pepparkakor* in Sweden and *Brunkager* in Denmark, both variants often prepared during the Christmas holidays. Local recipes include spices such as ginger, cinnamon, and cloves, and these cookies are often cut into festive shapes such as stars, hearts, and gingerbread men.

Pepparkakor from Sweden

Danish Brunkager

Italy, with its *Panforte*, shows how gingerbread can be integrated into local culture by using typically

Mediterranean ingredients such as almonds, hazelnuts, and candied fruits. *Panforte* is often consumed during the holiday season and is a cherished gift due to its long shelf life and rich flavors.

The United Kingdom also has a well-established gingerbread tradition, notably with the gingerbread men mentioned earlier. These little man-shaped biscuits have become a symbol of British holidays, often decorated with colorful icing. The tradition of making gingerbread houses has also taken root, allowing families to gather and build and decorate these gingerbread houses, an activity that celebrates both creativity and conviviality.

Outside of Europe, gingerbread has also found its place. In the United States, gingerbread is a staple of the holiday season, with gingerbread house competitions becoming popular community events. American recipes often have a local twist, incorporating ingredients like molasses and additional spices.

Gingerbread, through its many variations and adaptations, is a testament to the richness of cultural exchanges and the ability of culinary traditions to transcend borders. Each version of gingerbread tells a unique story, blending the flavors and customs of the region that adopted it, and continues to evolve over time.

The Gingerbread House Competition in San Francisco

Historical Anecdotes and Legends

Gingerbread, as an ancient and revered pastry, is surrounded by numerous fascinating historical anecdotes and legends that have helped shape its reputation over the centuries.

One of the most famous legends is the origin of the gingerbread man. It is said that Queen Elizabeth I of England had a habit of surprising her distinguished guests by presenting them with gingerbread cookies shaped in their likeness. These carefully decorated cookies were presented at royal banquets, adding a touch of whimsy and flattery that greatly pleased her guests.

In Germany, another legend tells the story of a knight returning from the Crusades, who brought back the recipe for gingerbread. He shared it with the bakers of Nuremberg, who then perfected the recipe using the precious spices they received through trade routes. This story, although romantic, illustrates the importance of the Crusades in introducing Eastern spices to Europe.

Gingerbread is also linked to important historical figures. For example, it is said that Napoleon Bonaparte, during his military campaigns, always carried gingerbread for his soldiers. He believed that this treat, thanks to its energetic and preservative properties, maintained the morale and strength of his troops. This practice helped popularize gingerbread as a military provision.

Another interesting anecdote concerns the Abbey of Saint Gall in Switzerland. The monks of this abbey, renowned for their pastry skills, created a gingerbread recipe enriched with butter and milk, rare ingredients at the time. This luxurious version of gingerbread was reserved for religious celebrations and distinguished guests, reinforcing the status of gingerbread as an exceptional treat.

The legends surrounding gingerbread are not limited to Europe. In China, "honey cake," a local variant, is associated with healing rituals. It is believed that this cake, thanks to its spices and honey, has medicinal properties capable of fortifying the body and mind. This belief reflects the importance of natural ingredients and spices in traditional Chinese medicine.

Gingerbread has also found its place in literature and art. European fairy tales, such as the Brothers Grimm's "Hansel and Gretel," feature gingerbread houses, symbols of temptation and magic. These stories have helped cement gingerbread in the collective imagination, transforming it into a symbol of sweetness and wonder.

Through these anecdotes and legends, gingerbread appears not only as a delicious pastry but also as a silent witness to the history and beliefs of different cultures. Each story, each legend, adds a layer of richness to this timeless treat, making it even more precious to those who savor it.

In exploring the history of gingerbread, it is essential to understand the crucial role of spices. These precious ingredients, coming from all corners of the world, not only flavor and enrich gingerbread but also tell a rich story of discoveries and cultural exchanges. Let us now dive into the world of spices to discover their origins, production, and impact on this timeless delicacy.

2 THE SPICES OF GINGERBREAD

History of Spices in Cooking

Spices have played a central role in the evolution of cuisine through the ages. Since Antiquity, they were prized not only for their flavors but also for their medicinal properties. The Egyptian, Greek, and Roman civilizations used spices such as cinnamon, ginger, and cloves to enhance the flavor of their dishes and for religious rituals. Spices were also a symbol of wealth and prestige, transported over long distances via perilous trade routes.

Spices such as cinnamon and ginger were already mentioned in ancient texts, used both to flavor foods and for their medicinal virtues. The Egyptians used them in the mummification process for their preservative properties. The Greeks and Romans incorporated them into their dishes and remedies, considering them precious treasures.

Spices were transported on long and dangerous trade routes, such as the Silk Road, connecting the East to the West. These routes were essential for the diffusion of spices and their integration into cuisines around the world. Camel caravans and merchant ships were loaded with these precious goods, traveling across arid deserts and tumultuous seas.

Spices profoundly influenced the culinary cultures of the regions where they were introduced. In Europe, they revolutionized medieval cuisine by adding rich and complex flavors to dishes. They were also used to mask the taste of foods that were no longer fresh, a common practice at a time when preservation techniques were limited.

Common Spices Used in Gingerbread

Gingerbread derives its unique flavor from a blend of carefully selected spices. The key ingredients include cinnamon, ginger, cloves, nutmeg, and star anise. Each spice contributes a distinct note, creating a harmony of spicy and comforting flavors. Let's examine each of these spices in detail and their roles in the gingerbread recipe.

Cinnamon

Cinnamon, with its sweet and warm aroma, is an essential spice in gingerbread. It comes from the inner bark of trees from the *Cinnamomum genus*. The cinnamon sticks are dried and then ground into a fine powder. Cinnamon brings a sweet and spicy flavor that enhances the taste of other ingredients. In Alsace, for example, cinnamon is a key ingredient in *Bredele*, small Christmas cookies.

Cinnamon Sticks

From a health perspective, cinnamon is rich in antioxidants, which help combat free radicals in the body. It also has anti-inflammatory properties that can reduce pain and inflammation.

Ginger

Ginger, with its spicy and lemony notes, adds depth and warmth to the flavor of gingerbread. Used in the form of powder or freshly grated ginger, it is essential for providing that characteristic spicy sensation. Ginger is also known for its medicinal properties, particularly for aiding digestion. In England, gingerbread men are popular ginger-based cookies, often decorated for Christmas.

Ginger

From a health perspective, ginger is recognized for its beneficial effects on the digestive system. It helps relieve nausea, improves digestion, and, thanks to its anti-inflammatory properties, can reduce the symptoms of colds and flu.

Cloves

Cloves, with their intense and slightly bitter flavor, are used in small quantities to balance the flavors of gingerbread. They are the dried flower buds of the clove tree. Their powerful aroma can be overpowering, so they should be used sparingly. In Germany, cloves are often added to recipes for *Lebkuchen*, a traditional variety of gingerbread.

Cloves

Good to know: cloves can be used for their antiseptic and analgesic properties. They are effective in relieving toothaches and can also help improve digestion and reduce inflammation.

Nutmeg

Freshly grated nutmeg adds a warm and slightly sweet note to gingerbread. It is the kernel of the seed from the fruit of *Myristica fragrans*. Nutmeg should be used freshly grated to achieve the best aroma. In Scandinavia, nutmeg is commonly used in various pastries and Christmas dishes.

Nutmeg

In herbal medicine, nutmeg is known for its relaxing effects and can help improve sleep quality. It is also used to relieve pain and digestive disorders.

Star Anise

Star anise, with its sweet and slightly peppery taste, complements the spice blend of gingerbread. It is often used whole to infuse liquids or ground into a powder for a uniform mix. Star anise adds an exotic and aromatic touch. In France, star anise is often used in mulled wine recipes, which pairs well with gingerbread during the winter season.

Star Anise

Origin and Production of Gingerbread Spices

The spices used in gingerbread come from different regions of the world. Cinnamon originates from Sri Lanka, ginger from India, and cloves from the Moluccas in Indonesia. These tropical regions offer the ideal conditions for growing these aromatic spices.

Spice cultivation requires specific climatic conditions. For example, cinnamon is cultivated on trees that need to be hand-peeled, while ginger is harvested by digging up the rhizomes. Harvesting spices is often a manual process that requires great expertise.

Once harvested, the spices are dried in the sun or using modern dehydration methods. This process is crucial for preserving their aromas and properties. Some spices, like cloves, are also smoked to intensify their flavor.

Spices were transported over long distances via historic trade routes, such as the Silk Road, connecting the East to the West. These routes were essential for the dissemination of spices and their integration into cuisines worldwide.

3 GINGERBREAD MAKING AND RECIPES

Basic Ingredients and Their Roles

Gingerbread is an ancient delicacy whose recipe has evolved over the centuries. However, some basic ingredients remain constant, playing a crucial role in the unique texture and taste of this pastry. In this section, we will explore the essential ingredients of gingerbread and their importance in preparing this timeless delight.

Flour

Flour forms the base of the gingerbread dough. Traditionally, rye flour is used, which gives a dense texture and a slightly tangy taste. However, nowadays, many recipes also use wheat flour, which offers a lighter and fluffier texture. The quality of the flour is essential to achieve homogeneous and well-structured dough.

Honey

Honey is a key ingredient in gingerbread, not only for its natural sweetness but also for its ability to retain moisture, ensuring a soft texture. Honey provides a depth of flavor that sugar cannot replicate. Additionally, depending on the variety of honey used (flower honey, chestnut honey, etc.), gingerbread can present different aromas, adding to its complexity.

Spices

Spices are the soul of gingerbread. A typical blend includes cinnamon, ginger, cloves, nutmeg, and star anise. The previous chapter has already extensively covered these ingredients.

Sugar

Although honey is the primary sweetener, sugar is also often used in modern gingerbread recipes. Brown sugar or molasses are preferred for their rich taste and ability to caramelize, adding an extra depth of flavor to the gingerbread. Sugar also contributes to the dough's structure, allowing for even baking and a pleasant texture.

Leavening Agents

Leavening agents, such as baking powder or baking soda, are essential to give gingerbread its light and airy texture. These ingredients allow the dough to rise during baking, creating a tender and fluffy crumb. Without these agents, gingerbread would be too dense and compact.

Liquids

Liquids such as milk, water, or orange juice are used to hydrate the dough and mix the ingredients homogeneously. The choice of liquid can also influence the final taste of the gingerbread. For example, milk provides a creamy richness, while orange juice adds a fruity and tangy note that can balance the sweetness of honey and sugar.

Fats

Fats, such as butter or oil, play a crucial role in the texture of gingerbread. They help bind the ingredients together and contribute to the tenderness of the dough. Butter is often preferred for its rich flavor, while oil can offer a lighter and sometimes softer option.

Role of Ingredients in Texture and Taste

Each ingredient in gingerbread plays a specific role in creating this unique pastry. Flour and leavening agents determine the structure and lightness of the dough. Honey and sugar provide sweetness and depth of flavor, while spices create the distinctive aromatic profile of gingerbread. Liquids ensure the necessary hydration for homogeneous dough, and fats contribute to the tenderness and soft texture of the finished product.

Different Preparation Methods

The preparation of gingerbread has evolved over time, from ancient artisanal methods to more sophisticated modern techniques. In this section, we will explore the different methods of preparing gingerbread, highlighting traditional techniques, modern innovations, and the advantages and disadvantages of each approach.

Traditional Preparation Methods

Traditional methods of preparing gingerbread date back centuries, with recipes passed down from generation to generation. Here is an overview of the typical steps in a traditional recipe:

- Dough Preparation

  Traditional gingerbread dough often begins by mixing warm honey with spices. The honey is gently heated until it becomes liquid, allowing the spices to fully release their aromas. Then, the flour is gradually added, followed by other ingredients such as eggs and fats.

- Dough Resting

  A distinctive feature of traditional preparation is the resting time of the dough. After being mixed, the dough is often left to rest for several hours or even overnight. This rest period allows the flavors to develop and the dough to hydrate evenly.

- Baking

  The rested dough is then rolled out and cut into shapes before being baked at a low temperature. Slow baking ensures a soft texture and a slightly caramelized crust. In some recipes, the dough is baked in wooden molds, which adds a subtle aroma and traditional shape.

Modern Techniques and Innovations

With the evolution of culinary technology, modern methods of preparing gingerbread have introduced innovations that simplify the process and offer new creative possibilities:

- Automated Mixing

  Kitchen robots and electric mixers allow the dough to be prepared quickly and uniformly. This automation reduces preparation time and ensures perfect consistency.

- Pre-Mixed Ingredients

  Ready-to-use gingerbread mixes, available commercially, simplify preparation by reducing the number of steps. These mixes often include flour, spices, and leavening agents, requiring only the addition of wet ingredients.

- Quick Baking

  Modern convection ovens and baking sheets allow for faster and more even baking. This technology ensures that gingerbread is perfectly baked, with a soft texture and a golden crust.

- Creative Variations

Modern techniques also allow for creative variations, such as adding dried fruits, nuts, or chocolate chips to the dough. Pastry chefs also experiment with innovative shapes and decorations, using cookie cutters and colorful icings.

Comparison of Different Methods

Each method of preparing gingerbread has its advantages and disadvantages:

- Traditional Methods

  Advantages: Rich and authentic flavors, soft texture, respect for traditions.

  Disadvantages: Longer preparation time, need to let the dough rest, more labor-intensive.

- Modern Techniques

  Advantages: Speed and ease of preparation, uniform consistency, creative possibilities.

  Disadvantages: May lack the authenticity of traditional methods, dependence on technology.

Whether you choose a traditional or modern method, preparing gingerbread offers a rewarding and delicious experience. Traditional techniques allow you to connect with the history and authentic flavors of gingerbread, while modern innovations provide flexibility and creativity to explore new culinary dimensions.

Different Recipes

Gingerbread is a pastry rich in history and flavors, with recipes that vary according to regions and local traditions. In this section, we will explore some of the most iconic traditional recipes, highlighting regional differences and historical variations that have shaped this sweet delight.

Classic Gingerbread Recipe

The classic gingerbread recipe is characterized by its rich and spicy flavor, soft texture, and long shelf life. Here is a traditional recipe that captures the essence of this timeless delight:

Ingredients:

- 250g rye flour
- 250g honey
- 100g brown sugar
- 10g baking soda
- 2 eggs
- 100ml milk
- 1 teaspoon ground cinnamon
- 1 teaspoon ground ginger
- 1/2 teaspoon ground cloves
- 1/2 teaspoon grated nutmeg
- 1 pinch of salt

Instructions:

1. Preheat the oven to 180°C (350°F).

2. Heat the honey in a saucepan until it becomes liquid.
3. In a large bowl, mix the flour, sugar, baking soda, spices, and salt.
4. Add the eggs, milk, and liquid honey to the dry ingredients and mix until you get a smooth batter.
5. Pour the batter into a buttered and floured cake tin.
6. Bake in the oven for about 45 minutes, or until a toothpick inserted in the center comes out clean.
7. Let cool before removing from the tin and enjoying.

France: *"Pain d'Épices de Dijon"* Recipe

Dijon gingerbread is one of the most famous variations in France. Traditionally made with rye flour, honey, and spices, it is known for its dense and moist texture. The people of Dijon often add candied orange zest for an extra touch of flavor and aroma.

Ingredients:

- 250g rye flour
- 200g honey
- 100g brown sugar
- 1 teaspoon baking soda
- 1 teaspoon ground cinnamon
- 1/2 teaspoon ground ginger
- 1/2 teaspoon ground cloves
- 100ml milk
- 100g candied orange zest

Instructions:

1. Preheat the oven to 180°C (350°F). Preheat your oven so it reaches the ideal temperature when you place the batter in it.
2. Heat the honey. In a saucepan, heat the honey over low heat until it becomes liquid. This helps it incorporate better with the other ingredients.
3. Mix the dry ingredients. In a large bowl, mix the rye flour, brown sugar, baking soda, cinnamon, ginger, and cloves. Make sure the mixture is well combined.
4. Add the milk and honey. Pour the milk and heated honey into the flour and spice mixture. Mix until you get a smooth batter. If the batter is too thick, add a little more milk.

Pain d'épices de Dijon

5. Incorporate the candied orange zest. Add the candied orange zest to the batter and mix well to distribute it evenly.
6. Pour the batter into a mold. Butter and flour a cake tin. Pour in the batter and smooth the surface with a spatula.
7. Bake in the oven. Place the tin in the oven and bake for about 45 minutes, or until a toothpick inserted in the center comes out clean.
8. Let it cool. Let the gingerbread cool in the tin for a few minutes before removing it to a wire rack to cool completely.

Germany: *Lebkuchen* Recipe

German *Lebkuchen* is a type of gingerbread often enjoyed during the Christmas season. It is soft and spiced, usually decorated with a sugar glaze or covered in chocolate. Typical ingredients include cinnamon, ginger, cloves, and cardamom.

Ingredients:

- 300g flour
- 200g honey
- 150g brown sugar
- 2 eggs
- 1 teaspoon baking soda
- 1 teaspoon ground cinnamon
- 1/2 teaspoon ground ginger
- 1/2 teaspoon ground cloves
- 1/4 teaspoon ground cardamom
- 100g dried fruits (raisins, almonds, hazelnuts)

Lebkuchen

Instructions:

1. Preheat the oven to 180°C (350°F).
2. In a saucepan, heat the honey over low heat until it becomes liquid. This makes it easier to incorporate with the other ingredients.
3. Mix the dry ingredients. In a large bowl, mix the flour, brown sugar, baking soda, cinnamon, ginger, cloves, and cardamom. Ensure the spices are well distributed.
4. Add the eggs and liquid honey to the flour and spice mixture. Mix well until you get a homogeneous dough.
5. Incorporate the dried fruits and zest. Add the raisins, almonds, hazelnuts, and, if desired, lemon zest and candied cherries. Mix well to evenly distribute the fruits in the dough.

6. Shape the cookies. Using a spoon, place mounds of dough on a baking sheet lined with parchment paper. Slightly flatten each mound to give them a cookie shape.

7. Bake the sheet in the oven for about 15 to 20 minutes, or until the cookies are golden brown. Watch the baking process carefully to prevent burning.

8. Let the *Lebkuchen* cool on a wire rack before enjoying. You can store them in an airtight container to keep them soft.

Optional: Decoration

9. Sugar Glaze: Mix 100g powdered sugar with 2-3 tablespoons of lemon juice. Apply the glaze to the cooled cookies and let it harden.

10. Chocolate Coating: Melt 200g dark chocolate in a double boiler. Dip the cooled cookies in the melted chocolate and let them harden on a wire rack.

Piernik: Traditional Polish Gingerbread

Piernik is a traditional Polish gingerbread, often prepared for the holiday season. Dense and rich, it is flavored with honey, cinnamon, ginger, and cloves, and can be filled with jam or covered in chocolate.

Ingredients:

- 300g flour

- 250g honey
- 100g brown sugar
- 2 eggs
- 100g butter
- 1 teaspoon baking soda
- 1 teaspoon ground cinnamon
- 1/2 teaspoon ground ginger
- 1/2 teaspoon ground cloves
- 1/4 teaspoon ground nutmeg
- 100g jam (plum, raspberry)

Instructions:

1. Preheat the oven to 180°C (350°F). Preheat your oven so it reaches the ideal temperature when you place the batter in it.
2. Heat the honey and butter. In a saucepan, heat the honey and butter over low heat until the mixture is liquid and homogeneous. Let it cool slightly.
3. Mix the dry ingredients. In a large bowl, mix the flour, brown sugar, baking soda, cinnamon, ginger, cloves, and nutmeg. Ensure the spices are well distributed in the flour.
4. Add the eggs and the honey-butter mixture. Add the eggs to the flour and spice mixture. Then, incorporate the melted honey and butter mixture. Mix well until you get a smooth batter.
5. Pour the batter into a mold. Butter and flour a cake tin. Pour in the batter and smooth the surface with a spatula.
6. Bake in the oven. Place the tin in the oven and bake for about 45 to 50 minutes, or until a toothpick inserted in the center comes out clean.

Watch the baking process to prevent the gingerbread from burning.

7. Let cool and fill. Let the *Piernik* cool in the tin for a few minutes before removing it to a wire rack to cool completely. Once cooled, you can cut it in half lengthwise and fill it with jam or melted chocolate, then reassemble the two halves.

Piernik

Optional: Decoration

8. For a finishing touch, you can cover the *Piernik* with melted chocolate or a sugar glaze. For the glaze, mix 100g powdered sugar with 2-3 tablespoons of lemon juice and spread it over the cake.

United States: Gingerbread Cookies Recipe

In the United States, gingerbread often takes the form of small spiced cookies called gingerbread cookies. Popular during the Christmas holidays, these cookies are often decorated with colorful icing and candies.

Ingredients:

- 350g flour
- 150g brown sugar
- 100g butter
- 1 egg
- 200g molasses
- 1 teaspoon baking soda
- 1 teaspoon ground cinnamon
- 1 teaspoon ground ginger
- 1/2 teaspoon ground cloves
- 1/4 teaspoon ground nutmeg
- 1 pinch of salt

Instructions:

1. Preheat the oven to 180°C (350°F). Preheat your oven so it is ready to receive the cookies once the dough is prepared.
2. Create the butter and sugar mixture. In a large bowl, beat the butter and brown sugar together until creamy and smooth. You can use an electric mixer to make this step easier.
3. Add the egg and molasses. Incorporate the egg and molasses into the butter and sugar mixture. Mix well until all ingredients are fully integrated.

4. Mix the dry ingredients. In another bowl, mix the flour, baking soda, cinnamon, ginger, cloves, nutmeg, and salt. Make sure the spices are well distributed in the flour.

5. Combine the mixtures. Gradually add the flour mixture to the wet ingredients. Mix until you get a homogeneous dough. If the dough is too soft, you can refrigerate it for 30 minutes to firm it up a bit.

6. Roll out the dough and cut out the cookies. On a lightly floured surface, roll out the dough to a thickness of about 0.5 cm. Use cookie cutters to cut out shapes of your choice (gingerbread men, stars, trees, etc.).

7. Place the cookies on a baking sheet. Place the cut-out cookies on a baking sheet lined with parchment paper, leaving some space between them to prevent sticking during baking.

8. Bake in the oven. Bake the cookies for about 8 to 10 minutes, or until the edges begin to turn golden. The cookies will still be slightly soft when they come out of the oven but will harden as they cool.

9. Let cool and decorate. Let the cookies cool on a wire rack. Once cooled, you can decorate them with icing and candies if desired.

Icing Preparation (Optional):

10. Mix 200g powdered sugar with 2-3 tablespoons of milk or lemon juice until you get a smooth consistency. Transfer the icing to a piping bag or a plastic bag with a corner cut off, and decorate the cookies as you like.

Gingerbread cookies

United States: Gingerbread Cake Recipe

Gingerbread cake is another popular variant in the United States, often served warm with whipped cream or ice cream. Soft and spiced, it is perfect for winter evenings.

Ingredients:

- 250g flour
- 100g brown sugar
- 100g butter
- 1 egg
- 250ml milk
- 200g molasses
- 1 teaspoon baking soda
- 1 teaspoon ground cinnamon
- 1 teaspoon ground ginger
- 1/2 teaspoon ground cloves
- 1/4 teaspoon ground nutmeg
- 1 pinch of salt

Instructions:

1. Preheat the oven to 180°C (350°F). Preheat your oven so it is ready to receive the cake once the batter is prepared.
2. Butter and flour a pan. Butter and flour a loaf pan or a 20x20 cm square pan to prevent the cake from sticking.
3. Mix the dry ingredients. In a large bowl, sift together the flour, baking soda, cinnamon, ginger, cloves, nutmeg, and salt. Mix well to evenly distribute the spices.

4. Prepare the butter and sugar mixture. In another bowl, beat the butter and brown sugar together until creamy and smooth. You can use an electric mixer to make this step easier.

5. Add the egg. Incorporate the egg into the butter and sugar mixture, mixing well until the mixture is light and fluffy.

6. Add the molasses and milk. Add the molasses to the mixture and mix well. Then, stir in the milk until all ingredients are well integrated.

7. Combine the mixtures. Gradually add the flour mixture to the wet ingredients, mixing until you get a smooth and homogeneous batter. Be careful not to overmix to avoid making the cake too dense.

Gingerbread cake

8. Pour the batter into the prepared pan and smooth the surface with a spatula.
9. Bake in the oven. Place the pan in the oven and bake for about 45 to 50 minutes, or until a toothpick inserted in the center of the cake comes out clean. Watch the baking process carefully to prevent the cake from burning.
10. Let it cool. Let the cake cool in the pan for a few minutes before removing it to a wire rack to cool completely.
11. Serve. Serve the gingerbread cake as is, or with icing, whipped cream, or a scoop of vanilla ice cream for extra indulgence.

Russia: *Pryaniki* Recipe

Pryaniki is a Russian version of gingerbread, often filled with jam or caramel and covered with a sweet glaze. It is enjoyed year-round and is especially popular during holidays.

Ingredients:

- 300g flour
- 200g honey
- 100g brown sugar
- 2 eggs
- 100g butter
- 1 teaspoon baking soda
- 1 teaspoon ground cinnamon
- 1/2 teaspoon ground ginger
- 1/2 teaspoon ground cloves

- Jam or caramel for filling

Instructions:

1. Preheat the oven to 180°C (350°F).
2. Heat the honey and butter. In a saucepan, heat the honey and butter over low heat until the mixture is liquid and homogeneous. Let it cool slightly.
3. Mix the dry ingredients. In a large bowl, mix the flour, brown sugar, baking soda, cinnamon, ginger, cloves, and nutmeg. Ensure the spices are well distributed.
4. Add the eggs and the honey-butter mixture. Add the eggs to the flour and spice mixture. Then, incorporate the melted honey and butter mixture. Mix well until you get a smooth dough.
5. Shape the cookies. Divide the dough into small portions and form balls. Slightly flatten each ball to form disks. If you wish to fill them, make a small depression in the center of each disk and add a small amount of jam or caramel, then cover with another disk of dough, sealing the edges well.
6. Place the cookies on a baking sheet. Place the formed cookies on a baking sheet lined with parchment paper, leaving some space between them to prevent sticking during baking.
7. Bake in the oven. Bake the cookies for about 10 to 12 minutes, or until they are lightly golden. The cookies will still be a bit soft when they come out of the oven but will harden as they cool.

8. Let cool. Let the *Pryaniki* cool on a wire rack. If desired, you can decorate them with a sugar glaze.

Glaze Preparation (Optional):

9. Mix 200g powdered sugar with 2-3 tablespoons of water or lemon juice until you get a smooth consistency. Dip the top of the cooled cookies into the glaze and let dry on a wire rack.

Pryaniki

Dutch Gingerbread: *Speculaas*

Speculaas is a Dutch variant of gingerbread, often molded into decorative shapes and enjoyed during the Saint Nicholas season. It is flavored with a unique spice blend called *speculaaskruiden*.

Ingredients:

- 250g flour
- 150g brown sugar
- 150g butter
- 1 egg
- 1 teaspoon baking soda
- 1 tablespoon *speculaaskruiden* (a blend of cinnamon, nutmeg, cloves, ginger, cardamom)
- 1 pinch of salt

Instructions:

1. Preheat the oven to 180°C (350°F). Preheat your oven so it is ready to receive the cookies once the dough is prepared.
2. Create the butter and sugar mixture. In a large bowl, beat the butter and brown sugar together until creamy and smooth. You can use an electric mixer to make this step easier.
3. Add the egg. Incorporate the egg into the butter and sugar mixture, mixing well until the mixture is light and fluffy.
4. Mix the dry ingredients. In another bowl, mix the flour, baking soda, *speculaaskruiden*, and salt. Ensure the spices are well distributed in the flour.
5. Combine the mixtures. Gradually add the flour mixture to the wet ingredients. Mix until you get homogeneous dough. If the dough is too soft, you can refrigerate it for 30 minutes to firm it up a bit.
6. Roll out the dough and cut out the cookies. On a lightly floured surface, roll out the dough to a thickness of about 0.5 cm. Use cookie cutters to

cut out shapes of your choice or form traditional rectangles.

7. Place the cookies on a baking sheet. Place the cut-out cookies on a baking sheet lined with parchment paper, leaving some space between them. If desired, you can decorate the cookies with sliced almonds.

8. Bake in the oven. Bake the cookies for about 10 to 12 minutes, or until the edges begin to turn golden. The cookies will still be slightly soft when they come out of the oven but will harden as they cool.

9. Let cool. Let the *Speculaas* cool on a wire rack before enjoying. You can store them in an airtight container to keep them crisp.

Speculaas

Historical Variations of the Recipe

Over the centuries, the gingerbread recipe has evolved, reflecting cultural influences and the ingredients available at each period. For example, in the Middle Ages, gingerbread was often prepared with pepper, a precious spice at the time, in addition to traditional spices.

- Medieval Gingerbread

  A medieval version of gingerbread could include ingredients such as black pepper, cumin, and anise, in addition to honey and classic spices. This ancient recipe was spicier and less sweet than modern versions.

- Renaissance Gingerbread

  During the Renaissance, gingerbread became sweeter with the addition of refined sugar complementing the honey. Recipes from this period often included candied fruits and nuts, adding texture and varied flavors to the pastry.

Traditional gingerbread recipes are as diverse as they are delicious, with each region and era contributing to this rich culinary heritage. Whether you prefer the classic version, regional variations, or historical recipes, gingerbread offers endless possibilities to delight the taste buds and celebrate traditions.

Modern Recipes and Innovations

Over time, gingerbread recipes have evolved, incorporating modern techniques and culinary innovations. Pastry chefs and cooking enthusiasts are constantly exploring new ways to reinvent this classic by experimenting with innovative ingredients and cooking methods. In this section, we will examine some of these modern recipes and the innovations that bring a new dimension to gingerbread.

Recent Innovations in Gingerbread Making

- **Use of Alternative Ingredients**
  - o **Alternative flours**: Increasingly, modern gingerbread recipes use gluten-free flours such as rice flour, almond flour, or coconut flour. This allows for the creation of gingerbread versions suitable for people with intolerances or food allergies.
  - o **Natural sweeteners**: Refined sugar is often replaced by natural sweeteners like maple syrup, agave syrup, or coconut sugar. These alternatives bring unique flavors and additional nutritional benefits.
- **Advanced Baking Techniques**
  - o **Vacuum cooking**: This cooking technique allows gingerbread to be baked at low temperatures, ensuring a perfectly moist and uniform texture. Vacuum also preserves the aromas of the spices, offering a more intense taste experience.

o **Use of silicone molds**: Silicone molds allow for the creation of complex and detailed shapes, transforming gingerbread into true culinary works of art. They also facilitate unmolding and reduce the risk of breakage.

Contemporary Chef Recipes

Matcha Green Tea Gingerbread

Ingredients:

- 250g wheat flour
- 200g honey
- 100g brown sugar
- 10g matcha green tea powder
- 2 eggs
- 100ml milk
- 1 teaspoon baking soda
- 1 teaspoon ground cinnamon
- 1/2 teaspoon ground ginger
- 1/2 teaspoon ground cloves
- 1 pinch of salt

Instructions:

1. Preheat the oven to 180°C (350°F).
2. Heat the honey in a saucepan until it becomes liquid.
3. In a large bowl, mix the flour, sugar, matcha powder, baking soda, spices, and salt.

4. Add the eggs, milk, and liquid honey to the dry ingredients and mix until you get a smooth batter.
5. Pour the batter into a buttered and floured loaf pan.
6. Bake in the oven for about 45 minutes, or until a toothpick inserted in the center comes out clean.
7. Let cool before removing from the pan and enjoying.

Orange and Cranberry Gingerbread

Ingredients:

- 250g wheat flour
- 200g honey
- 100g brown sugar
- 100g dried cranberries
- Zest of 2 oranges
- 2 eggs
- 100ml orange juice
- 1 teaspoon baking soda
- 1 teaspoon ground cinnamon
- 1/2 teaspoon ground ginger
- 1/2 teaspoon ground cloves
- 1 pinch of salt

Instructions:

1. Preheat the oven to 180°C (350°F).
2. Heat the honey in a saucepan until it becomes liquid.

3. In a large bowl, mix the flour, sugar, baking soda, spices, and salt.

4. Add the eggs, orange juice, orange zest, and liquid honey to the dry ingredients and mix until you get a smooth batter.

5. Fold in the dried cranberries.

6. Pour the batter into a buttered and floured loaf pan.

7. Bake in the oven for about 45 minutes, or until a toothpick inserted in the center comes out clean.

8. Let cool before removing from the pan and enjoying.

Modern Presentation and Tasting Ideas

- **Gingerbread in Verrines:**

    Cut the gingerbread into small cubes and layer them with whipped cream and fresh fruit in small glasses. This elegant presentation is perfect for receptions and festive desserts.

Gingerbread in Verrines

- **Glazed Gingerbread**

  Dip slices of gingerbread into melted chocolate and let them cool on a wire rack. The chocolate adds a delicious and crunchy touch.

- **Gingerbread Toasts**

  Serve slices of gingerbread with soft cheese, such as brie or camembert, and a drizzle of honey. This sweet-and-salty combination is perfect for appetizers.

Gingerbread and Goat Cheese Toast

Modern recipes and innovations in gingerbread making show that this traditional pastry can be reinvented in countless ways. Whether through the use of alternative ingredients, advanced baking techniques, or creative presentations, gingerbread continues to captivate palates and inspire chefs worldwide.

Throughout the pages of this chapter, we have explored the richness and diversity of gingerbread recipes in depth. We have discovered the basic ingredients and their essential roles, the different preparation methods, whether traditional or modern, as well as regional variations and recent innovations. These recipes, rooted in history and adapted to contemporary tastes, attest to the popularity and versatility of gingerbread.

However, gingerbread is not just about its recipes. It is also deeply embedded in cultural and culinary traditions around the world. The occasions to enjoy gingerbread are numerous, whether it's family celebrations, religious festivals, or simple moments of shared indulgence.

In the next chapter, we will delve into the various traditions associated with gingerbread. We will explore how this pastry is integrated into celebrations and festivities across different eras and cultures. We will also discover the symbols and meanings attributed to it, as well as the personal memories and stories that make it such a special dessert.

4 TRADITIONS AND CELEBRATIONS

Gingerbread is a delicious pastry, but it is also imbued with deep cultural and festive meanings. Throughout the ages, this sweet treat has transcended its simple nature to become a symbol of conviviality, celebration, and tradition. Around the world, gingerbread plays a central role in many religious holidays and special occasions, bringing together family and friends around its comforting flavor.

Gingerbread and Religious Festivals

Gingerbread is closely associated with several religious holidays, notably Christmas. This time of year is particularly marked by the preparation and enjoyment of gingerbread in various forms. The Christmas tradition surrounding gingerbread finds its roots in medieval European customs, where it was given as a gift and used to decorate homes and Christmas trees.

Christmas and the Gingerbread Tradition

At Christmas, gingerbread often takes the form of decorative houses, gingerbread men, and trees. These festive shapes are delightful to eat, but they also add a touch of magic to Christmas decorations. The making of gingerbread houses, in particular, has become a traditional family activity. Children and adults alike participate in creating these structures, using candies, icing, and colorful decorations to embellish their creations.

Gingerbread men are also an integral part of Christmas celebrations. Their making and decoration are often moments of shared joy, where everyone can unleash their creativity. In Germany, the famous *Lebkuchen* are often prepared and enjoyed during the Advent season, contributing to the festive and warm atmosphere of Christmas markets.

Other Holidays and Celebrations

Although Christmas is the holiday most closely associated with gingerbread, other religious and cultural occasions also incorporate this pastry. For example, in Poland, *Piernik* is often prepared for Easter and other religious holidays. This dense and spiced gingerbread is sometimes decorated with religious motifs and served at festive meals.

In some cultures, gingerbread is also present at weddings and year-end celebrations. In Russia, *Pryaniki* are often given as gifts during New Year and Orthodox Christmas celebrations, symbolizing prosperity and happiness for the coming year.

Gingerbread holds a special place in many religious and festive traditions around the world. Whether in the form of decorated houses, fun gingerbread men, or delicious spiced loaves, it brings joy and conviviality to all celebrations. By delving into the history and traditions of gingerbread, we discover a wealth of flavors as well as a deep connection to our cultural and familial heritage.

Family Traditions around Gingerbread

Family traditions play a central role in perpetuating the art of gingerbread making. These traditions are often passed down from generation to generation, with each family adding its unique touch to the recipe and preparation methods. Exploring family traditions around gingerbread reveals a world rich in rituals, shared memories, and moments of conviviality.

Family Preparation Rituals

The preparation of gingerbread in the family is a ritual that often begins well before the holidays. It's a time when family members gather to measure, mix, and shape the dough, creating precious memories. The kitchen fills with the enchanting aromas of honey, cinnamon, ginger, and cloves, heralding the arrival of the festive season.

In many families, making gingerbread houses is an annual tradition. These houses, decorated with colorful candies and sweet icing, become festive centerpieces proudly displayed on Christmas tables. Children love to participate in the decoration, unleashing their creativity and imagination. For adults, this ritual offers an opportunity to reconnect with the traditions of their childhood.

Making gingerbread men is another popular tradition. Each family member can decorate their own gingerbread man with chocolate chips, raisins, candies, and icing. This simple yet fun activity strengthens family bonds and adds a personal touch to the celebration.

Sharing Recipes and Passing on Traditions

Gingerbread recipes are often family treasures, carefully preserved and passed down through generations. Each family has its own version, with specific ingredients and unique preparation techniques. These recipes are more than just culinary instructions; they are living links to the past, with each bite evoking memories of ancestors and shared moments.

In some families, sharing the gingerbread recipe is a rite of passage. Grandparents teach grandchildren the secrets of perfect dough, balanced spices, and ideal baking. This transfer of knowledge helps preserve the family heritage and ensures that traditions continue to live on through the generations.

The family recipe book, often handwritten and stained with flour and honey, is a true treasure. It contains annotations, modifications, and additions made over time, reflecting the evolving tastes and preferences of the family. Each year, new pages can be added, documenting culinary innovations and variations experimented by family members.

<u>Moments of Sharing and Conviviality</u>

Gingerbread making is much more than a simple culinary activity; it is a moment of sharing and conviviality. Working together in the kitchen, family members share stories, laughter, and conversations. These moments strengthen family bonds and create lasting memories.

Children, in particular, love participating in gingerbread preparation. They learn basic cooking skills, develop their creativity, and take pleasure in seeing their creations take shape and being enjoyed. For parents and grandparents, it is an opportunity to impart values of teamwork, patience, and pride in a job well done.

Once the gingerbread is baked and decorated, the enjoyment continues with the tasting. The family gathers around the table, sharing the fruits of their labor. Conversations often revolve around childhood memories, past holidays, and future plans. Gingerbread, with its comforting flavor and familiar aromas, becomes the centerpiece of these moments of sharing.

Gingerbread Shapes and Decorations

The shapes and decorations of gingerbread are as varied as the cultures and traditions that surround them. Each shape tells a story, evokes memories, and adds a festive touch to celebrations. In this first part, we will explore the history and techniques of making gingerbread houses, one of the most iconic forms of this pastry.

Gingerbread Houses

Gingerbread houses have become an essential Christmas tradition in many homes around the world. Their origin dates back to 19th-century Germany, inspired by the Grimm Brothers' fairy tale "Hansel and Gretel," where the children discover a gingerbread house in the forest. Since then, these decorative houses have become synonymous with creativity and festivity during the holiday season.

- History and Origin of Gingerbread Houses

    The idea of building gingerbread houses is closely linked to German Christmas markets. These markets, which date back to the Middle Ages, were places where artisans sold treats and festive items. The first gingerbread houses were often elaborate representations of homes and castles, decorated with candies and icing. They were given as gifts and displayed as centerpieces during Christmas celebrations. Over time, the tradition of gingerbread houses spread to other European countries and North America. Each region added its own touches and variations, but the spirit of creativity and sharing remained the same.

- Construction and Decoration Techniques

    Building a gingerbread house may seem intimidating, but with the right techniques and a bit of patience, it is a fun and rewarding activity for the whole family. Here are the basic steps to create a gingerbread house:

1. Preparing the Dough

   Use a gingerbread dough recipe that yields a firm and easy-to-handle dough. Roll out the dough on a lightly floured surface to a thickness of about 0.5 cm.

2. Cutting the Pieces

   Use cardboard templates to cut out the different parts of the house: walls, roof, doors, and windows. Make sure the pieces are straight and even to facilitate assembly.

3. Baking the Pieces

   Bake the gingerbread pieces in a preheated oven at 180°C (350°F) until they are golden and firm to the touch. Let them cool completely before handling.

4. Assembling the House

   Use royal icing (a mixture of powdered sugar and egg white) as "glue" to assemble the pieces. Start with the walls, holding them in place until the icing hardens. Then add the roof and other decorative elements.

5. Decoration

   Let your creativity run wild to decorate the house. Use candies, cookies, chocolate chips, dried fruits, and colored icing to embellish your creation. Children love participating in this step, adding their personal touch to the decoration.

- Gingerbread House Competitions

Gingerbread house competitions have become popular in many communities and schools, adding a spirit of friendly competition to this festive tradition. These competitions encourage creativity and ingenuity, with each participant aiming to impress with innovative designs and elaborate decorations. Some competitions include categories for different age levels, allowing everyone to participate, from children to adults.

The gingerbread houses displayed at these competitions are often complex works of art, depicting fairy tale scenes, Christmas villages, and even famous landmarks. Judges evaluate the creations based on criteria such as originality, design complexity, and quality of decoration.

After exploring gingerbread houses, let's continue our discovery of the festive shapes of this iconic pastry. Gingerbread men and other decorative shapes, such as trees and stars, also bring a touch of magic and creativity to holiday celebrations.

Gingerbread Men

Gingerbread men, known as gingerbread men, are another popular form of this pastry. Their cheerful appearance and spicy flavor make them a favorite among children and adults during the holidays.

- Significance and Popularity of Gingerbread Men

  The origin of gingerbread men dates back to the court of Queen Elizabeth I of England, who had biscuits made in the shape of her most important guests. Since then, these man-shaped biscuits have become festive symbols associated with conviviality and fun. Gingerbread men are often decorated with colorful icing, candies, and raisins to represent eyes, buttons, and other details. This decoration activity is a popular family tradition, allowing everyone to create their own unique gingerbread man.

- Recipes and Decoration Techniques

1. Preparing the Dough

   Use a classic gingerbread recipe to prepare the dough. Roll it out on a lightly floured surface to a thickness of about 0.5 cm.

2. Cutting the Gingerbread Men

   Use gingerbread man cookie cutters to cut out the biscuits. Place the cut-out shapes on a baking sheet lined with parchment paper.

3. Baking

   Bake the biscuits in a preheated oven at 180°C (350°F) for about 10 to 12 minutes, or until they are slightly golden. Let them cool completely before decorating.

4. Decorating

Prepare royal icing with powdered sugar and egg white. Use piping bags to draw the facial features, clothing, and buttons. Add candies, chocolate chips, and dried fruits to personalize your gingerbread men.

Christmas Trees and Other Festive Shapes

In addition to houses and gingerbread men, gingerbread can be shaped into various other festive forms such as trees, stars, hearts, and bells. These shapes are often used to decorate Christmas trees or as edible gifts.

- Using Molds and Cutters

  Cookie cutters are essential tools for creating precise and uniform gingerbread shapes. They come in a variety of shapes and sizes, allowing for an assortment of cookies for all festive occasions. Silicone molds can also be used to create detailed reliefs and patterns.

- Decoration Ideas for Different Shapes

1. Christmas Trees

   Decorate gingerbread trees with green icing to represent branches. Add colorful sugar beads to mimic Christmas ornaments and sprinkle with powdered sugar for a snowy effect.

2. Stars

   Use white or gold icing to decorate the stars. Add edible glitter for a sparkling and festive touch.

3. Hearts

   Gingerbread hearts can be decorated with romantic designs and given as gifts. Use red and white icing to create delicate patterns.

4. Bells

   Decorate the bells with silver or gold icing. Add snowflake patterns and small candies for a festive appearance.

- Symbolism of Festive Shapes

  Each gingerbread shape has a special meaning and adds a symbolic dimension to the celebrations. Christmas trees symbolize eternity and rebirth, while stars represent light and hope. Hearts are symbols of love and affection, often given to express warm feelings.

Gingerbread in Popular Culture

Beyond its delicious flavors and festive traditions, gingerbread has also found an important place in popular culture. It appears in fairy tales, legends, and even contemporary media, showcasing its lasting impact and popularity throughout the ages.

Gingerbread in Fairy Tales and Legends

One of the most famous fairy tales featuring gingerbread is "Hansel and Gretel" by the Brothers Grimm. In this story, the two children discover a house made entirely of gingerbread, candy, and sweets in the forest. This house, though tempting and magical, belongs to an evil witch. The tale captures the imagination of both children and adults, making gingerbread a symbol of temptation and wonder. Other European legends also mention gingerbread. For example, in some regions of France and Germany, gingerbread was said to have protective properties and bring good luck. Heart-shaped biscuits, often hung in homes during the holidays, were believed to protect the inhabitants and bring happiness and prosperity.

References in Media and Literature

Gingerbread continues to fascinate and inspire contemporary creators. It frequently appears in movies, TV shows, and books, especially during the Christmas season. Films like "Shrek" popularized the character of the Gingerbread Man, adding a humorous and endearing touch to this classic figure. Cookbooks, magazines, and culinary shows regularly feature segments on gingerbread, exploring its many variations and decoration techniques. Television baking competitions, such as "The Great British Bake Off," often include gingerbread challenges, highlighting the creativity and ingenuity of amateur and professional bakers.

Influence of Gingerbread in Modern Traditions

In modern culture, gingerbread has become a symbol of festive spirit and generosity. Gingerbread decorating workshops are common in schools and community centers during the holidays, offering children and adults a chance to gather and share joyful moments. Christmas markets, particularly in Europe, showcase stalls brimming with gingerbread in all shapes and forms. These markets attract millions of visitors each year, becoming must-visit destinations for those seeking to experience the magic of Christmas.

Modern Adaptations and Artistic Creations

The impact of gingerbread extends beyond traditional holidays. Artists and designers often use gingerbread as inspiration for their creations. Gingerbread sculptures, edible artworks, and ephemeral installations have become popular expressions in exhibitions and artistic events. International gingerbread competitions, like the "National Gingerbread House Competition" in the United States, highlight complex and impressive artworks, pushing the boundaries of pastry and decoration. These events celebrate innovation and creativity while honoring the age-old traditions of gingerbread.

Gingerbread, with its roots deeply embedded in history and traditions, continues to captivate the collective imagination. Its influence extends far beyond the kitchen, finding a place in fairy tales, legends, media, and the arts. Throughout the ages, gingerbread remains a symbol of warmth, generosity, and creativity, bringing people together around shared memories and new traditions.

As we have explored the various traditions and cultural representations of gingerbread, it is time to delve into another fascinating aspect of this pastry: its moments of enjoyment and health benefits. Gingerbread, besides being delicious, offers numerous nutritional advantages thanks to its natural ingredients and spices. In the next chapter, we will discover the best times to savor gingerbread, ideal accompaniments, and the dietary aspects that make it a treat as beneficial as it is tasty.

5 TASTING AND NUTRITION

Gingerbread, with its rich and spicy flavors, is a pastry that embodies conviviality, sharing, and family traditions. Its enjoyment extends to various occasions throughout the year, always bringing a touch of comfort and pleasure. In addition to its delicious taste, gingerbread offers health benefits thanks to its natural and nutritious ingredients. Each ingredient in gingerbread, such as honey, cinnamon, ginger, and cloves, provides significant nutritional benefits. By incorporating these elements into a balanced diet, gingerbread can contribute to overall better health.

Best Times to Enjoy Gingerbread

Gingerbread is versatile and can be enjoyed at different times and for various occasions. Here are some of the best occasions to savor this treat:

Holidays and Celebrations

Gingerbread is an undisputed star of the holiday season. At Christmas, it is omnipresent on festive tables, whether in the form of decorative houses, gingerbread men, or spiced cakes. Its presence brings a warm and festive atmosphere, recalling childhood memories and moments shared with family. Additionally, gingerbread is also appreciated during other religious and cultural holidays. For example, in Germany, *Lebkuchen* are popular during Advent, while in Poland, *Piernik* is often prepared for Easter and other celebrations.

Special Occasions

Gingerbread can also be served during special occasions throughout the year, such as birthdays, weddings, and receptions. It can be used as a main dessert or as a decorative element, bringing a touch of elegance and tradition to the event. For example, a gingerbread wedding cake, decorated with delicate icing patterns, can be a unique and delicious alternative to traditional wedding cakes.

Moments of Relaxation and Conviviality

Beyond major occasions, gingerbread is also perfect for moments of relaxation and conviviality. It can be enjoyed with a cup of tea or coffee during an afternoon break, or served as a comforting snack on a cold winter's day. Gingerbread, with its warming spices, is ideal for creating a cozy and soothing atmosphere.

Picnics and outdoor gatherings are other perfect occasions to savor gingerbread. Easy to transport and share, it makes for a practical and delicious snack that appeals to all ages.

In summary, gingerbread is a versatile pastry that adapts to a multitude of occasions. Whether celebrating holidays, marking special events, or simply enjoying a moment of relaxation, gingerbread is always a comforting and tasty choice. Its nutritional benefits also make it a healthier treat option, adding an extra dimension to its appeal.

Ideal Accompaniments

Gingerbread, with its rich and complex flavors, pairs perfectly with a variety of drinks and accompaniments. Whether for a quiet snack, a festive dessert, or a treat with friends, choosing the right accompaniments can enhance the taste experience. In this first part, we will explore the beverages that perfectly complement gingerbread.

Beverages

- Tea

  Tea is a classic accompaniment to gingerbread. The subtle and sometimes floral notes of tea can balance the intense spices of gingerbread. Here are some suggestions:

  o **Black Tea**: A robust black tea like Darjeeling or Earl Grey pairs perfectly with the warm spices of gingerbread.

- o **Green Tea**: For a lighter option, green tea, such as Sencha or Matcha, offers a delicate flavor that pleasantly contrasts with the richness of gingerbread.
- o **Spiced Tea**: A Chai or a Christmas spiced tea, with its notes of cinnamon, cardamom, and ginger, enhances the flavors of gingerbread for a harmonious experience.

- Coffee

Coffee, with its characteristic bitterness, creates a delightful contrast with the sweetness and spices of gingerbread. Here's how to pair coffee with gingerbread:

- o **Espresso**: An intense espresso highlights the aromas of gingerbread, offering a powerful combination of flavors.
- o **Coffee Latte**: The creamy sweetness of a latte balances the spices of gingerbread, creating perfect harmony.
- o **Flavored Coffee**: A coffee flavored with vanilla, hazelnut or cinnamon can add an extra dimension to the gingerbread tasting experience.

- Milk

Milk, due to its natural sweetness and creamy texture, is an excellent choice for pairing with gingerbread, especially for children. Here are some variations:

- o **Warm Milk**: A glass of warm milk, possibly sweetened with a bit of honey, creates a comforting pairing with gingerbread.
- o **Almond Milk**: For a dairy-free alternative, almond milk brings a sweet and slightly nutty flavor that pairs well with the spices.
- o **Honey and Spiced Milk**: Heat some milk with a spoonful of honey and a pinch of cinnamon or nutmeg for a warm and soothing drink.

- Mulled Wine

  Mulled wine, often prepared with spices similar to those in gingerbread, is another festive drink that pairs perfectly with this pastry. Here's how to prepare and enjoy it:

  - o **Red Wine**: Use a quality red wine, such as a Merlot or Cabernet Sauvignon, as the base for your mulled wine.
  - o **Spices**: Add cinnamon sticks, cloves, star anise, orange zest, and a bit of sugar or honey.
  - o **Heating**: Heat the wine with the spices without bringing it to a boil to preserve the subtle aromas. Serve warm in heat-resistant mugs.

Beverages play an essential role in the gingerbread tasting experience. Whether it's tea, coffee, milk, or mulled wine, each beverage offers a unique way to savor and appreciate the complex flavors of this pastry. By choosing the right accompaniments, you can enrich and diversify your tasting moments, transforming each bite into a true sensory delight.

Gingerbread lends itself to a multitude of sweet and festive accompaniments, allowing for the creation of refined and delicious desserts. In this second part, we will explore complementary desserts and presentation suggestions that elevate gingerbread, transforming it into a true culinary work of art.

Complementary Desserts

- Whipped Cream

    The lightness and sweetness of whipped cream perfectly contrast with the dense texture and spices of gingerbread. Here are some ideas to incorporate it:

    o **Vanilla Whipped Cream**: Add a hint of vanilla to the whipped cream for an extra aroma that pairs well with the spices.
    o **Spiced Whipped Cream**: For an original touch, add a pinch of cinnamon or nutmeg to the whipped cream.
    o **Mascarpone Whipped Cream**: Mix mascarpone with whipped cream for a richer and creamier version.

- Ice Cream

    The freshness of ice cream pleasantly contrasts with the warmth of gingerbread spices. Here are some combination suggestions:

- o **Vanilla Ice Cream**: A scoop of vanilla ice cream served with a warm slice of gingerbread creates a perfect balance between hot and cold.
- o **Salted Caramel Ice Cream**: The richness of salted caramel adds depth of flavor to each bite of gingerbread.
- o **Ginger Ice Cream**: For a harmonious taste experience, try ginger ice cream that accentuates the spicy notes of gingerbread.

- Fruits

  Fresh and stewed fruits bring a touch of lightness and freshness to gingerbread. Here are some ideas to pair them:

  - o **Apple Compote**: The sweetness of apple compote pairs perfectly with the spices of gingerbread, creating a comforting dessert.
  - o **Candied Oranges**: Candied oranges add a citrus note and a crunchy texture that complement gingerbread well.
  - o **Red Berries**: Red berries like raspberries and blackberries, with their natural acidity, balance the richness of gingerbread.

Presentation Suggestions

- Festive Dishes

  Gingerbread can be elegantly presented for holidays and special occasions. Here are some presentation suggestions:

- o **Tasting Platter**: Arrange slices of gingerbread on a platter with various accompaniments such as fruits, creams, and ice creams, allowing guests to create their own combinations.
- o **Individual Mini Cakes**: Prepare mini gingerbread cakes for a neat and practical presentation, perfect for buffets or receptions.
- o **Plated Dessert**: Serve a warm slice of gingerbread with a scoop of vanilla ice cream, a dollop of whipped cream, and fruit compote, garnished with mint leaves and citrus zest.

- Elegant Presentation for Special Occasions

For special occasions, transform gingerbread into a sophisticated dessert. Here are some ideas:

- o **Gingerbread Verrines**: Alternate layers of crumbled gingerbread, whipped cream, and fruits in verrines for an elegant and easy-to-enjoy dessert.
- o **Gingerbread Toasts**: Serve lightly toasted gingerbread slices topped with soft cheese, honey, and dried fruits for a gourmet appetizer.
- o **Gingerbread Cake**: Make a gingerbread cake by layering slices of gingerbread with chocolate ganache and whipped cream, decorated with fresh fruits and nuts.

Accompaniments and presentations for gingerbread offer numerous possibilities to enhance the tasting experience. Whether paired with whipped cream, ice cream, fruits, or presented in elegant and festive ways, gingerbread can be transformed into an exquisite dessert that will delight the taste buds and amaze guests.

Nutritional Aspects and Benefits

Gingerbread, in addition to being a delicious treat, is also appreciated for its nutritional benefits. The natural ingredients used in its preparation provide various health advantages, making this pastry a healthier choice compared to other more processed desserts. In this first part, we will explore the benefits of the main ingredients in gingerbread.

<u>Natural Ingredients and Their Benefits</u>

- Honey

  Honey is one of the key ingredients in gingerbread, and it is renowned for its numerous health benefits:

  - **Antioxidants**: Honey contains antioxidants that help protect the body against free radicals and reduce the risk of chronic diseases.
  - **Antibacterial Properties**: Due to its antibacterial properties, honey can help soothe sore throats and improve digestive health.

77

- **Natural Energy**: Honey is an excellent source of quick and natural energy, ideal for a revitalizing snack.

- Spices

  The spices used in gingerbread, such as cinnamon, ginger, cloves, and nutmeg, offer a range of health benefits:

  - **Cinnamon**: Cinnamon is known for its anti-inflammatory and antioxidant properties. It can help regulate blood sugar levels and improve heart health.
  - **Ginger**: Ginger is often used for its anti-nausea and anti-inflammatory effects. It can also help relieve muscle pain and improve digestion.
  - **Cloves**: Cloves have antimicrobial and antioxidant properties. They can help reduce inflammation and improve oral health.
  - **Nutmeg**: Nutmeg is rich in antioxidants and has anti-inflammatory properties. It can also help improve digestion and relieve pain.

- Flour

  The flour used in gingerbread can vary, but rye flour is often preferred for its texture and nutritional benefits:

  - **Fiber**: Rye flour is high in fiber, which helps improve digestion and maintain a feeling of fullness for longer.

- **Vitamins and Minerals**: It contains B vitamins, iron, and magnesium, which are essential for energy production and overall health.
- **Low Glycemic Index**: Compared to wheat flour, rye flour has a lower glycemic index, which helps regulate blood sugar levels.

- Brown Sugar

  Brown sugar, used in some gingerbread recipes, provides natural sweetness while offering additional minerals:

  - **Molasses**: Brown sugar contains molasses, which is a source of calcium, potassium, iron, and magnesium.
  - **Energy**: Like honey, brown sugar provides quick energy, useful for times when an energy boost is needed.

The natural ingredients in gingerbread not only provide rich and complex flavors but also offer numerous health benefits. By incorporating ingredients like honey, spices, and rye flour, gingerbread becomes a nutritious treat that can be enjoyed guilt-free. In the next section, we will explore the nutritional values of gingerbread and possible adaptations for different dietary needs.

After exploring the benefits of gingerbread's natural ingredients, let's now look at the overall nutritional values of this pastry and the possible adaptations to meet different dietary requirements.

Nutritional Values

Gingerbread, thanks to its natural ingredients, offers an interesting nutritional composition. Here is an overview of the main nutrients that can be found in a slice of gingerbread:

- **Calories:** A slice of gingerbread typically contains between 150 and 200 calories, making it a moderately caloric snack.
- **Carbohydrates:** Gingerbread is rich in complex carbohydrates from flour and natural sugars like honey and brown sugar. These carbohydrates provide sustained energy.
- **Fiber:** Due to the use of rye or whole wheat flour, gingerbread can contain a significant amount of fiber, essential for digestion.
- **Protein:** While not a major source of protein, gingerbread does contain a small amount from eggs and flour.
- **Fats:** The fats in gingerbread primarily come from added fats like butter or oil, as well as eggs. These fats contribute to the moist texture and rich taste.
- **Vitamins and Minerals:** Gingerbread contains essential vitamins and minerals, including B vitamins, iron, calcium, and magnesium, thanks to ingredients like rye flour, honey, and spices.

Comparison with Other Sweets

Gingerbread stands out from other pastries and sweet desserts due to its more balanced nutritional profile. Unlike highly processed cakes and cookies, gingerbread uses natural ingredients that offer health benefits. The spices not only add flavor but also provide antioxidant and anti-inflammatory properties.

Adaptations for Specific Diets

To meet the needs of different diets, gingerbread recipes can be adapted. Here are some suggestions for gluten-free, sugar-free, and vegan versions:

- Gluten-Free Recipes

    o **Alternative Flours**: Use gluten-free flours like rice flour, almond flour, or coconut flour instead of wheat or rye flour.
    o **Natural Binders**: Add binders like xanthan gum or guar gum to achieve a texture similar to traditional gingerbread.

- Sugar-Free Recipes

    o **Natural Sweeteners**: Replace brown sugar and honey with natural sweeteners like agave syrup, maple syrup, or coconut sugar, which have a lower glycemic index.
    o **Sugar Substitutes**: Use sugar substitutes like erythritol or xylitol, which do not affect blood sugar levels.

- Vegan Recipes

  o **Flax or Chia Eggs**: Replace eggs with flax or chia eggs (1 tablespoon of ground flax or chia seeds mixed with 3 tablespoons of water per egg).
  o **Plant-Based Milk**: Use plant-based milk like almond milk, soy milk, or coconut milk instead of cow's milk.
  o **Vegan Butter**: Replace butter with coconut oil or vegan margarine.

Gingerbread, with its natural ingredients and nutritional benefits, is a pastry that can be enjoyed by everyone, even those following specific diets. By adapting the recipes to be gluten-free, sugar-free, or vegan, gingerbread can continue to be a comforting and healthy treat for all sweet lovers.

As we explored this chapter, we discovered that gingerbread is not only a delicious pastry but also a nutritious option thanks to its natural and healthful ingredients. Whether through the benefits provided by honey, spices, or whole flours, gingerbread stands out with a balanced and comforting nutritional profile. Additionally, the various accompaniments and possible adaptations make this treat accessible to everyone, regardless of dietary restrictions.

The various accompaniment suggestions, from beverages to complementary desserts, highlighted the numerous ways to savor gingerbread. Whether for festive moments, special occasions, or moments of relaxation, gingerbread always brings a touch of warmth and conviviality.

As we have explored the tasting and dietary aspects of gingerbread, it is time to look towards the future of this iconic pastry. In the next chapter, we will discuss emerging trends and innovations shaping the future of gingerbread.

We will discover how new flavors and modern techniques are redefining this culinary tradition while respecting its historical heritage. We will also explore the environmental and ethical aspects related to the production of gingerbread ingredients and how these considerations influence contemporary practices.

Continuing our journey through the world of gingerbread, we will delve into the art of passing down traditions, examining how new generations are preserving and innovating in the preparation of this timeless treat. Join us in the next chapter to discover the exciting prospects awaiting gingerbread and how it will continue to delight palates for years to come.

6 THE FUTURE OF GINGERBREAD

Gingerbread, with its roots deeply embedded in history and traditions, has managed to traverse the ages while adapting to cultural and culinary evolutions. At the dawn of the 21st century, this iconic pastry continues to captivate sweet lovers thanks to its ability to innovate while respecting its rich heritage. In this chapter, we will explore the emerging trends shaping the future of gingerbread, as well as the technological innovations and environmental and ethical considerations influencing its production and consumption.

The importance of innovation within tradition cannot be overstated. By integrating new flavors, techniques, and sustainable practices, gingerbread can continue to evolve and adapt to the tastes and values of future generations. This ability to innovate while respecting traditions helps preserve the cultural richness of gingerbread while ensuring its contemporary relevance.

Emerging Trends

Current culinary trends strongly influence how gingerbread is prepared, presented, and enjoyed. Here are some of the new flavors and combinations gaining popularity:

<u>New Flavors and Combinations</u>

One of the most notable trends is the integration of exotic and unexpected flavors into gingerbread recipes. Pastry chefs and cooking enthusiasts are constantly exploring new combinations to offer unique taste experiences. Here are some examples:

- **Exotic Spices:** In addition to traditional spices like cinnamon, ginger, and cloves, other spices such as cardamom, Sichuan pepper, and turmeric are increasingly used to add depth and complexity to gingerbread recipes.
- **Tropical Fruits:** Ingredients like mango, pineapple, and passion fruit are incorporated into gingerbread recipes to bring a touch of freshness and exoticism.
- **Aromatic Herbs:** Herbs such as rosemary, thyme, and lavender are used to add subtle and fragrant notes to gingerbread, creating novel and refined combinations.

Cardamom Seeds

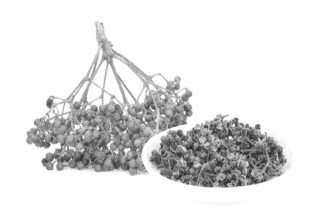

Sichuan Pepper

Turmeric

Technological Innovations in Pastry

Technological advances in the field of pastry open up new possibilities for the preparation and decoration of gingerbread. These innovations push the boundaries of creativity while improving the precision and efficiency of traditional techniques. Here are some of the most promising innovations:

- **Edible 3D Printing:** Using 3D printing to create decorations and structures in gingerbread allows for complex and personalized designs with unparalleled precision. This technology is particularly popular for artistic creations and pastry competitions.
- **Smart Cooking Appliances:** Ovens and kitchen robots equipped with smart sensors and precise temperature control functions enable uniform and optimal baking of gingerbread. These appliances also facilitate the preparation

of large quantities while ensuring consistent quality.

- **Advanced Preservation Techniques:** Innovations in preservation techniques, such as freeze-drying and vacuum packaging, extend the shelf life of gingerbread without compromising its quality and freshness. These methods are especially useful for products intended for export or online sales.

Emerging trends and technological innovations play a crucial role in the evolution of gingerbread. By integrating new flavors and adopting modern techniques, this traditional pastry continues to reinvent itself and captivate sweet lovers. In the next section, we will explore in more detail the modern preparation and decoration techniques shaping the future of gingerbread.

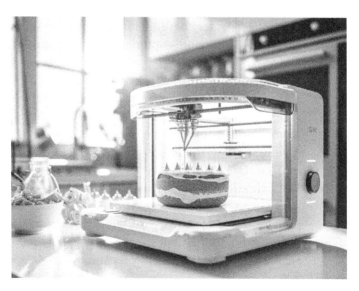

A 3D Food Printer

Modern Preparation and Decoration Techniques

With the evolution of technologies and culinary trends, the techniques for preparing and decorating gingerbread have significantly advanced. Both professional and amateur pastry chefs are exploring new methods to create gingerbread that is visually stunning and tastefully innovative.

Modern Preparation Techniques

The preparation techniques for gingerbread have been modernized through the use of advanced equipment and new culinary methods. Here are some of the most popular techniques:

- **Vacuum**: Vacuum cooking involves sealing the gingerbread ingredients in an airtight plastic bag and cooking them at a low temperature in a controlled water bath. This method ensures even cooking and optimal preservation of flavors and nutrients.
- **Fermentation**: Inspired by traditional bread-making techniques, gingerbread fermentation allows for the development of more complex flavors and a unique texture. This technique involves letting the dough rest for several hours or even days before baking.
- **Robotization**: Using culinary robots to mix, knead, and shape the dough makes it easier to prepare large quantities of gingerbread while maintaining consistent quality. Robots also enable precise and uniform preparations.

Modern Decoration Techniques

Gingerbread decoration has also benefited from technological advances and new pastry trends. Modern decoration techniques allow for the creation of elaborate and personalized designs. Here are some examples:

- **Airbrushing:** Airbrushing is a technique that involves spraying edible paint onto gingerbread using an airbrush gun. This method allows for creating color gradients, detailed patterns, and artistic effects on the surfaces of gingerbread.
- **Sugar Pastes and Fondants:** Sugar pastes and fondants are used to cover and decorate gingerbread. They enable the creation of intricate designs, figurines, and raised decorations. Pastry chefs also use cookie cutters and silicone molds to form precise patterns.
- **Royal Icing:** Royal icing remains a classic technique, but it is now used more creatively. Modern pastry chefs utilize different consistencies of royal icing to create 3D decorations, lace patterns, and complex ornaments. Royal icing can also be colored to add vibrancy and personalization to the creations.
- **Molding Techniques:** Silicone molds allow for creating detailed shapes and patterns with gingerbread. These molds can be used to make gingerbread houses, figurines, or complex decorations. Silicone molds offer great precision and make it easy to unmold without damaging the creations.

Influence of Current Culinary Trends

Current culinary trends also influence how gingerbread is prepared and decorated. Here are some trends impacting modern gingerbread:

- **Vegan and Gluten-Free Cuisine:** With the rise in popularity of vegan and gluten-free diets, many gingerbread recipes have been adapted to meet these needs. Egg substitutes, alternative flours, and natural sweeteners are used to create versions of gingerbread suitable for these specific diets.
- **Culinary Fusions:** Pastry chefs are exploring culinary fusions by combining gingerbread with elements from other culinary traditions. For example, pairing gingerbread with Asian flavors like matcha or yuzu creates new and exciting taste experiences.
- **Minimalism and Scandinavian Aesthetics:** The minimalist and clean aesthetic of Scandinavian cuisine also influences gingerbread decoration. Simple designs, natural colors, and geometric patterns are favored to create elegant and sophisticated creations.

Modern preparation and decoration techniques push the boundaries of creativity in gingerbread. By adopting innovative methods and drawing inspiration from current culinary trends, pastry chefs can create gingerbread that is both delicious and visually impressive. In the next section, we will explore the environmental and ethical impact of gingerbread production and the initiatives aimed at making this pastry more sustainable.

Environmental and Ethical Impact

Respect for the environment and ethical practices has become a major concern in the food industry. Gingerbread, as a traditional and beloved product, is not exempt from this trend. Sustainable and responsible production of this pastry can help preserve our planet while honoring artisanal traditions. In this first part, we will discuss the use of sustainable and fair-trade ingredients, as well as waste reduction and eco-friendly packaging.

Use of Sustainable and Fair-Trade Ingredients

One of the most effective ways to reduce the environmental impact of gingerbread is by using sustainable and fair-trade ingredients. Here are some practices and ingredient choices that promote more responsible production:

- **Organic and Local Honey:** Favoring organic and local honey reduces the carbon footprint associated with transportation and supports local beekeepers. Organic honey is produced without pesticides or chemicals, which benefits the environment and biodiversity.
- **Fair-Trade Spices:** Spices such as cinnamon, ginger, and cloves can be purchased from fair-trade certified producers. These certifications ensure fair working conditions and sustainable farming practices, thus supporting producer communities in developing countries.
- **Sustainable Flours:** Using flours from organic farming or ancient grains helps preserve biodiversity and reduce pesticide use. Local or

responsibly produced flours also limit the ecological footprint related to transportation.

Waste Reduction and Eco-Friendly Packaging

Waste management and the use of eco-friendly packaging are crucial aspects of sustainable gingerbread production. Here are some initiatives and practices to minimize environmental impact:

- **Compostable and Recyclable Packaging:** Using compostable or recyclable packaging for gingerbread products helps reduce plastic waste. Materials such as kraft paper, recycled cardboard, and biodegradable films are sustainable alternatives to traditional plastic packaging.
- **Reducing Food Waste:** Optimizing production processes to minimize food waste is essential. Leftover dough or pieces of gingerbread can be repurposed to create other products, such as gingerbread crumbs for desserts or bases for cheesecakes.
- **Zero Waste Initiatives:** Adopting a zero waste approach in gingerbread production involves reducing, reusing, and recycling as much as possible. This can include composting organic waste, reusing packaging materials, and implementing effective recycling programs.

Local and Seasonal Sourcing

Sourcing local and seasonal ingredients is another way to reduce the environmental impact of gingerbread production. Here are some benefits of this approach:

- **Reduction of Carbon Footprint:** Local sourcing reduces transportation distances, thereby lowering greenhouse gas emissions associated with logistics.
- **Support for Local Producers:** Buying from local producers strengthens the local economy and encourages sustainable farming practices.
- **Seasonal Fruits and Vegetables:** Using seasonal ingredients allows for the use of products at their peak in terms of freshness and flavor, while supporting more natural and environmentally friendly production cycles.

Using sustainable and fair-trade ingredients, reducing waste, and opting for eco-friendly packaging are crucial steps in making gingerbread production more environmentally friendly. By adopting these practices, producers can not only preserve the quality and authenticity of this traditional pastry but also contribute to protecting our planet. In the next section, we will further explore initiatives for responsible production and the importance of local and seasonal sourcing.

After exploring the importance of sustainable and fair-trade ingredients, as well as waste reduction and eco-friendly packaging, let's now focus on broader initiatives for responsible production and the importance of local and seasonal sourcing.

Initiatives for Responsible Production

Numerous initiatives aim to make gingerbread production more responsible and environmentally friendly. These initiatives involve sustainable farming practices, certifications, and awareness programs.

- **Sustainable Farming Practices:** Encouraging producers to adopt sustainable farming practices is essential for reducing environmental impact. This includes using eco-friendly cultivation techniques such as crop rotation, organic compost, and reducing chemical pesticides.
- **Environmental Certifications:** Certifications like organic farming, "Fair Trade," and "Rainforest Alliance" ensure that the ingredients used are produced responsibly. Gingerbread producers can obtain these certifications for their products, assuring consumers that their purchases support sustainable practices.
- **Awareness Programs:** Companies can launch awareness programs to educate consumers about the benefits of sustainable products and encourage them to make more responsible choices. This can include marketing campaigns, workshops, and community events focused on sustainability.

Importance of Local and Seasonal Sourcing

Sourcing local and seasonal ingredients is a key approach to reducing the ecological footprint of gingerbread production. Here are some additional benefits of this practice:

- **Fresher and Higher Quality**: Local and seasonal ingredients are often fresher and of higher quality because they are harvested at peak ripeness and do not need to travel long distances.

- **Support for the Local Economy**: Buying from local producers supports the regional economy and helps keep farms and producers in business.
- **Reduced Dependence on Imports**: By focusing on locally available ingredients, gingerbread producers can reduce their dependence on imports, which is especially important during global supply chain disruptions.

Community Initiatives and Partnerships

Community initiatives and partnerships can play a crucial role in promoting sustainability in gingerbread production. Here are some examples of such initiatives:

- **Agricultural Cooperatives:** Agricultural cooperatives allow local producers to pool their resources to sell their products collectively, reducing distribution costs and increasing their bargaining power. Cooperatives can provide high-quality ingredients to gingerbread producers at fair prices.
- **Partnerships with NGOs:** Companies can partner with NGOs working on sustainable development and fair agriculture projects. These partnerships can help promote responsible farming practices and raise consumer awareness of environmental issues.
- **Farmers' Markets:** Participating in local farmers' markets allows gingerbread artisans to sell their products directly to consumers, reducing the carbon footprint associated with distribution and strengthening ties with the local community.

Initiatives for responsible production and local and seasonal sourcing are essential elements for making gingerbread production more sustainable. By adopting these practices, producers can not only reduce their environmental impact but also support local economies and promote fair and sustainable farming practices. In the next section, we will explore the art of transmitting culinary traditions, examining how to preserve and renew gingerbread techniques and recipes for future generations.

The Art of Transmission

The Art of Transmission

The transmission of culinary traditions is essential for preserving the cultural heritage of gingerbread while allowing its evolution. Teaching techniques and recipes to new generations ensures that this beloved pastry continues to thrive and adapt to contemporary tastes. Here are some ways to pass on this art:

Preserving and Transmitting Traditions

- **Workshops and Pastry Classes**: Organizing workshops and pastry classes is an excellent way to pass down traditional gingerbread-making techniques. These practical sessions allow participants to discover the secrets of this pastry, learn authentic recipes, and understand the importance of ingredients.
- **Family Recipes**: Encouraging families to share their gingerbread recipes, often passed down

through generations, helps preserve these culinary treasures. Family recipe books, cooking gatherings, and community events are effective ways to celebrate and perpetuate these traditions.

- **Documentation and Publication**: Publishing cookbooks, articles, and videos on gingerbread preparation helps document and disseminate traditional techniques to a broad audience. Digital media, in particular, offers an accessible platform to share knowledge and skills.

Encouraging Creativity and Innovation in New Generations

- **Pastry Competitions**: Organizing pastry competitions focused on gingerbread stimulates creativity and innovation. These events allow amateur and professional bakers to showcase their unique creations and push the boundaries of tradition.
- **Educational Programs**: Integrating educational programs on baking into schools and culinary universities inspires young people to explore and experiment with gingerbread. Internships, research projects, and collaborations with experienced chefs offer valuable learning opportunities.
- **Social Media and Online Communities**: Social media and online communities are dynamic platforms for sharing ideas, recipes, and techniques. Young bakers can draw inspiration from others' creations, exchange tips and tricks, and find support for their projects.

Role of Culinary Schools and Pastry Workshops

- **Professional Training**: Culinary schools and baking workshops play a crucial role in transmitting culinary skills. Professional training programs provide a solid foundation in traditional techniques while encouraging innovation and creativity.
- **Partnerships with Artisans**: Collaborating with artisans and pastry experts allows students to benefit from the experience and knowledge of master bakers. These partnerships enrich learning and promote the exchange of know-how.
- **Internships and Apprenticeships**: Offering internships and apprenticeships in bakeries and pastry shops specializing in gingerbread allows students to gain practical experience and understand the challenges and opportunities of the profession.

As we have explored the history, traditions, recipes, innovations, and ethical considerations of gingerbread, it is clear that this pastry continues to evolve while staying true to its roots. Gingerbread, a symbol of conviviality and indulgence, embodies the richness of culinary traditions while adapting to contemporary tastes and values.

Invitation to Experiment and Innovate

We invite all cooking enthusiasts to experiment and innovate with gingerbread. Whether you are a professional baker, a passionate amateur, or simply someone who enjoys a good pastry, explore different recipes, techniques, and presentations to create your own unique versions of gingerbread. By perpetuating this tradition while adding your personal touch, you contribute to the preservation and enrichment of this culinary heritage.

CONCLUSION

Summary of Key Points

Throughout this book, we have delved into the fascinating world of gingerbread, a pastry rich in history, traditions, and flavors. We began by tracing its ancient origins and its development through the ages, highlighting the cultural influences that shaped its recipe and popularity. The spices, an essential ingredient in gingerbread, were examined in detail for their history and nutritional benefits.

We also discovered the various methods of making gingerbread and its different recipes, from traditional versions to modern innovations. The traditions and celebrations surrounding gingerbread were highlighted, revealing how this sweet treat is integrated into religious and family festivities worldwide. Finally, we explored the aspects of tasting and nutrition, as well as the environmental and ethical impact of gingerbread production.

Invitation to Discovery and Creativity

Gingerbread is not just a delicious pastry; it is also a symbol of conviviality, sharing, and culinary innovation. We invite you to continue exploring and experimenting with gingerbread in your own kitchen. Try different recipes, play with spices and ingredients, and feel free to add your personal touch. Whether you are a professional or an amateur, there are always new ways to reinvent this age-old tradition.

Preserving and Transmitting Traditions

Transmitting culinary traditions is essential for preserving our gastronomic heritage. Share your gingerbread recipes with your family and friends, participate in baking workshops, and document and publish your creations. By sharing your knowledge and skills, you contribute to perpetuating and enriching the tradition of gingerbread for future generations.

Looking to the Future

Gingerbread will continue to evolve and adapt to contemporary tastes and values. Emerging trends, technological innovations, and environmental considerations will play a key role in this evolution. By adopting sustainable practices and supporting local and fair trade producers, we can ensure that gingerbread remains an environmentally friendly and community-respectful treat.

In conclusion, gingerbread is much more than just a pastry. It is a journey through history, culture, and culinary creativity. We hope this book has inspired you and that you will enjoy creating and savoring gingerbread as much as we enjoyed writing these pages.

Made in the USA
Monee, IL
30 November 2024

71736683R00066